# THE APOSTLES' CREED

Nihil Obstat: Reverend Michael L. Diskin, Assistant Chancellor
Imprimatur: Most Reverend Thomas J. Olmsted, Bishop of Phoenix
Date: June 6, 2014

*Bart Tesoriero*
*Illustrated by Miguel D. Lopez*

catholic children's CLASSICS

ISBN 978-1-61796-142-7

Artwork and Text © 2014 Aquinas Kids, Phoenix, Arizona
Printed in China

# The Apostles' Creed

I believe in God, the Father almighty,
Creator of heaven and earth,
and in Jesus Christ, his only Son, our Lord,
who was conceived by the Holy Spirit,
born of the Virgin Mary,
suffered under Pontius Pilate,
was crucified, died, and was buried.

He descended into hell;
on the third day
he rose again from the dead;
he ascended into heaven,
and is seated at the right hand of
God the Father almighty;
from there he will come to judge
the living and the dead.

I believe in the Holy Spirit,
the holy catholic Church,
the communion of saints,
the forgiveness of sins,
the resurrection of the body,
and life everlasting. Amen.

# I believe in God, the Father almighty, Creator of heaven and earth,

In the beginning, a long, long time ago, before the world was made, before there was the sky, or the sun, or the moon, there was God.

You may ask, wasn't God lonely, since He alone is God and there are no other gods besides Him?

Well, the truth is, God is like a family! That's right. The one true God exists as three divine persons. A Holy Trinity (of persons)! This is a mystery that we cannot fully understand. God has revealed Himself as one God, but three divine persons: God the Father, God the Son, and God the Holy Spirit.

God was completely happy. In fact, He was so happy that He wanted to share His happiness with others. God wanted a bigger family, with whom He could share His love. And so God created angels and God created us!

First of all, God decided to make a place where men, women, and children could live. And so, God created the heavens and the earth. Then God created human beings. The Bible calls our first parents Adam and Eve. God made them in His image and likeness. God placed Adam and Eve in a beautiful paradise called the Garden of Eden. God looked at everything He had made, and He found it to be very good.

# And in Jesus Christ, His only Son, our Lord,

God told Adam and Eve that they could eat of the fruit of every tree in the Garden except for the tree of the knowledge of good and evil. He told them that if they ate of it, they would die.

One day, the devil came in the form of a snake to tempt Eve. Eve decided to eat of the forbidden fruit. She then gave some to Adam, who also ate it. When they ate the fruit, they realized they had displeased God by disobeying Him. They were separated from God in their hearts, and could no longer stay in the Garden. But God also promised in the fullness of time to send a Redeemer to save all people, a Savior who would be born of a woman.

God loves us so much that He sent His only Son to be with us, to show us how to live and to free us from sin. But how did God do that? How did God become a man? Read on.

# Who was conceived by the Holy Spirit, born of the Virgin Mary,

Adam and Eve had many descendants, who spread out over the face of the earth. However, as time passed, people sinned more and more and became wicked.

Many years after Adam and Eve, God called a holy man named Abram to leave his country and his father's family, and to go with his wife Sarai into a land that He would show him. God changed Abram's name to Abraham and Sarai's name to Sarah, and Abraham became the father of a great nation, the people of Israel.

Many, many years after Abraham, God sent the angel Gabriel to a town in Israel named Nazareth, to a virgin named Mary, who was engaged to Joseph. Gabriel said to Mary, "Hail, full of grace! The Lord is with you! Do not be afraid, Mary. You have found favor with God. Behold, you will conceive a son in your womb, and you shall call him Jesus. He will be great, the Son of the Most High God." Mary said, "I am the handmaid of the Lord. Let it be done unto me according to your word."

Joseph and Mary traveled to Bethlehem, and there, Mary gave birth to her son, Jesus. God kept His promise!

# Suffered under Pontius Pilate,

The birth of Jesus was celebrated by angels and shepherds, and Wise Men traveling from far distant lands. But not everyone welcomed the news. A jealous king named Herod ruled the people of Israel, and he sent soldiers to kill all the baby boys in Bethlehem. An angel warned Joseph, and he took Mary and Jesus and fled to Egypt.

After King Herod died, the family returned to Nazareth, where Jesus grew up. He learned His school lessons, and Joseph taught Him to work as a carpenter. At the age of 30, Jesus left home to begin His ministry. He taught the people about God, His Father. He preached the Good News to them. He healed them of their diseases and drove out evil spirits. Jesus even raised the dead!

Many people of Israel loved Jesus and rejoiced in Him. But not everyone accepted Him. Some rulers were jealous of Jesus and resented Him. They arrested Jesus and brought Him to Pontius Pilate, the Roman governor. Pilate had Jesus beaten and crowned with thorns.

# Was crucified, died and was buried.

Pilate then condemned Jesus to death. The soldiers laid a heavy cross on Jesus' shoulders and made Him carry it up to the Mount of Calvary, where He was to be crucified.

When they arrived at Calvary, the soldiers nailed Jesus to the cross. On top of the cross Pilate had written the words, "Jesus of Nazareth, King of the Jews." Jesus looked up to heaven from the cross, and prayed, "Father, forgive them, for they do not know what they are doing."

As Jesus hung on the cross, He saw His mother Mary standing at the foot of the cross, with His beloved apostle, John. Jesus said to His mother, "Woman, behold your son." Then to John Jesus said, "Behold your mother." Jesus then said, "I thirst!" Finally Jesus cried in a loud voice, "It is finished. Father, into Your hands I commit my spirit." And bowing His head, Jesus died.

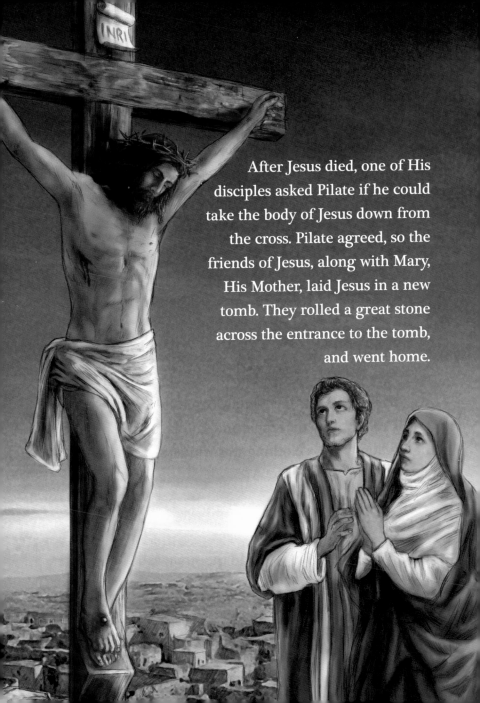

After Jesus died, one of His disciples asked Pilate if he could take the body of Jesus down from the cross. Pilate agreed, so the friends of Jesus, along with Mary, His Mother, laid Jesus in a new tomb. They rolled a great stone across the entrance to the tomb, and went home.

# He descended into hell; On the third day he rose again from the dead;

When Jesus died He went down to a place called *Sheol*, the place of the dead. All the people who had ever lived went to Sheol when they died. Those who had been good waited for a Redeemer. Jesus went to Sheol to free all the good people who had died before Him. He preached the Good News to all the souls imprisoned there.

Then, very early in the morning on the first day of the week, as soldiers were guarding the tomb, there was an earthquake! An angel of the Lord descended from heaven, approached the tomb, rolled away the stone, and sat upon it. He looked like lightening and his clothing was white as snow.

Mary Magdalene and some other women from Galilee had prepared spices and perfumed oils. At daybreak they brought the spices with them to the tomb. They had come to anoint the body of Jesus. They found the stone rolled away from the tomb, but when they entered, they did not find the body of Jesus. Suddenly they saw the angel. "Do not be afraid!" the angel said. "I know you are seeking Jesus. He is not here, for He is risen, just as He said. Go tell His disciples!"

# He ascended into heaven, and is seated at the right hand of God, the Father almighty;

In His death and Resurrection, Jesus delivered us from the power of sin and death. He opened the way to heaven. After His Resurrection, Jesus appeared to His disciples, who were overjoyed to find that He was alive!

Jesus stayed on the earth for forty days, speaking to His followers about the kingdom of God. Jesus was now ready to leave the earth and return to His Father in heaven.

Jesus told His apostles, "Do not depart from Jerusalem, but wait there for 'the promise of the Father' about which I have spoken to you. John baptized with water, but in a few days you will be baptized with the Holy Spirit. You will receive power when the Holy Spirit comes upon you. Then you will be My witnesses in Jerusalem, throughout Judea and Samaria, and to the ends of the earth."

After Jesus said this, He blessed His disciples, and ascended into heaven. As they were looking on, a cloud took Him out of their sight.

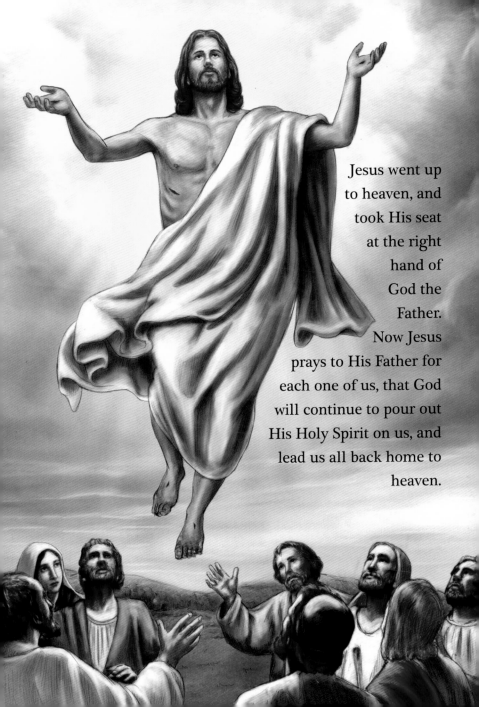

Jesus went up to heaven, and took His seat at the right hand of God the Father. Now Jesus prays to His Father for each one of us, that God will continue to pour out His Holy Spirit on us, and lead us all back home to heaven.

# From there He will come to judge the living and the dead.

Before Jesus went up to heaven, He promised His followers that one day He would return, to judge all people and to bring His faithful ones home to heaven, to be with Him forever.

We are living now in the "in-between" time, a time to prepare for the return of Jesus. He told us to always be ready, to keep our hearts open to Him. We do that by taking time every day to speak to Our Lord in prayer, by receiving the Sacraments, and by reading the Bible. We also keep our hearts pure by thinking of good things, by learning the truth, and by seeking to do our best. Jesus wants us to meet Him and to accept Him in our hearts. This will bring us joy. We will rejoice in Him.

God does not want us to hide the gifts He has given us, but to use our talents to do good in the world. Jesus told us to love others, especially those who are hungry and thirsty, those who are sick, without a home, or in prison.

As children, you can pray for these people, and you can be kind to your brothers and sisters and classmates. If you do this, you will be ready when Jesus returns, as the Judge of all people, both the living and the dead.

# I believe in the Holy Spirit,

The Holy Spirit is the third Person of the family of God that we call the Blessed Trinity. The Holy Spirit came down in tongues of fire on Mary and the Apostles on Pentecost. We receive the Holy Spirit in our Baptism and Confirmation. He opens our minds and our hearts to believe in Jesus. He helps us to become friends with God.

You know how good a cool drink of water feels on a hot day when you are really thirsty? The Holy Spirit is like a river of grace inside our hearts. The Holy Spirit gives us this living water because God wants us to always have His grace!

It is good to ask the Holy Spirit to come into our hearts every day. The Holy Spirit wants to give us gifts like wisdom, courage, and understanding. If we allow the Holy Spirit to live in us, He will grow fruit in us! Not the kind you eat, but the fruit of love, joy, peace, and goodness.

The Holy Spirit helps us to feel in our hearts that we are God's children and to feel the love that God our Father has for us. You belong to God. The Holy Spirit is our helper, who is by our side every day, all day, to help us in all that we do, and to teach us the truth.

# The Holy Catholic Church,

The word "church" means a community, a gathering of people. The Church is the family of all the children of God. The word "Catholic" means universal. Every person in the world is welcome to be a part of God's family.

The Church is holy, because through Baptism, each person in the Church has been made a child of God by the Holy Spirit. The Holy Spirit gives each of us a new heart, a heart open to God. Jesus is the Head of His Church, and all of us are part of His Body. The Church is the Body of Christ.

In the Church we feel the mercy of God. God's mercy and kindness fills our hearts with love. We belong to God! We also belong to one another. We are the family of God.

God has given to the Church everything we need to become holy. The Pope, our bishops, and priests teach us the truth of God and the good news of Jesus Christ. The Church gives us the sacraments and the Scriptures, which bring us God's grace. In the Church, God has also placed men and women who have given themselves to Jesus, whom we call religious brothers and sisters. They teach us and pray for us and help us to find God in our lives.

# The communion of saints,

The Church is a family. We are linked to one another by our Baptism. We are united in our hearts. However, we are not only a family of believers on earth. We also share a common union with all those who have died and have gone into heaven with Jesus. Together with them, we are members of the Communion of Saints. Those who have died and are being made ready for heaven are called the souls in purgatory.

Have you ever played on a team, maybe baseball, or football, or soccer? Have you ever sung in a chorus or choir? If you have, then you know that every person needs to do their part to help the team play well or to help the chorus put on a good concert.

All of us in the Church are on God's team! He has given each of us special gifts that no one else has. He wants each of us to share our gifts and to use them for the good of all. We need each other. Therefore, it is good to ask the saints in heaven to pray for you. It is also good to pray for the holy souls in purgatory that they can soon enter heaven and be with Jesus forever.

# The forgiveness of sins,

When you were baptized, a priest poured water over you. Very likely you already had your bath, so why did he do that? The Baptismal water stands for the cleansing of our souls from sin. Baptism makes us children of God, our Father, who forgives us of all our sins.

However, after we are baptized, we are still tempted to disobey God, and to say and do things that are not right. So what can we do when we sin? Can we still be forgiven? The answer is Yes! We believe in the forgiveness of sins.

After Jesus was raised from the dead, He appeared to His apostles. They were all together in a room, afraid that they would also be arrested and put to death, like Jesus. Suddenly Jesus appeared to them! "Peace be with you," He said. Then He breathed on them and said, "Receive the Holy Spirit. Whose sins you forgive are forgiven them, and whose sins you retain (do not forgive) are retained (not forgiven)." In this way, Jesus made a way for us to know that our sins are forgiven, which is celebrated in the Sacrament of Reconciliation (Penance).

This is a very joyful truth. Every time we tell God we are sorry, He forgives us and makes us clean again, through His Son, our Lord Jesus Christ.

# The resurrection of the body,

Each one of us has a body and a soul. Our bodies are what people see, on the outside. However, your soul is who you are on the inside. It is the you that lives in your body.

God is so great and so good that He sent His Son Jesus to become one of us, a human just like you. Jesus suffered and died for all of us, so that we could once again become children of God, our Heavenly Father. Jesus calls us to love God and obey Him today, on earth. However, some day each one of us will die. After we die, our bodies will one day return to dust. Our souls will not die. For those who have lived a holy life, our destiny will be to go to heaven and live with Jesus forever.

Jesus has some great news for us. He said, "I am the resurrection and the life." He promised that at the end of the world He would raise our bodies from the dead! When Jesus raises our bodies, He will change them from bodies that can die into new bodies that can never die, nor be hurt. Think of that! When you get your new body, you will never get sick! You will never get old. You will have a body that will be like the bodies that Jesus and Mary have, in heaven. The Church teaches this truth, and we thank God for this good news!

# And life everlasting. Amen.

Jesus said, "I have come that you might have life, and have it more abundantly." Indeed, God wants to give us life that will last forever. After we die here on earth, we will continue to exist. However, we have a choice as to where we will live.

All people who accept the love of God, our Father, and become His children will live in heaven someday. All people who refuse the grace that God offers them will be separated from God forever. They will be in hell.

Heaven is being with God, our Father, with Jesus and Mary and all the saints and angels. In heaven we will be completely happy. We will be completely free. We will love totally, and we will be totally loved. Jesus said that heaven will be like a great wedding feast, where we will all eat and drink and be happy forever.

On earth, we can see the beautiful things God has made, but we cannot see God, because He is too bright for us. In Heaven, we will see God as He is, so beautiful and so full of love. It will be awesome, and it will never end!

The final word in the Apostle's Creed is "Amen." *Amen* means, "Yes, it is so. I believe." Amen, we do believe!